PRAISE FOR WILD LEADERSHIP

"When it comes to leadership John is one of the best and smartest there is. Do yourself a favor and read *Wild Leadership* and implement the concepts in your own leadership journey. You'll be glad you did!"

—Jacob Morgan, 5x Best-Selling Author, Futurist, & Keynote Speaker. Founder of Future Of Work Leaders (Global CHRO Community). Focused on Leadership, The Future of Work, & Employee Experience

"I love the connection John, brilliant coach who I had the privilege to work with, makes between leadership and nature. The analogies really resonated with me and brought the concept of anchoring our authentic styles back to the natural world."

—Tecla Palli-Sandler, Chief People Officer, Vialto Partners

"John Sigmon's *Wild Leadership* is a wonderful exploration of the intersection between the natural world and leadership. Through his personal life experiences and business insights, John invites us to step beyond conventional leadership frameworks and embrace the wisdom, beauty, and timeless spirit of nature. By using practical exercises and reflections, John provides leaders at all levels with the tools to enhance our adaptability, resilience, and intuition. Wild Leadership is not just a book—it's an invitation to lead with heart, spirit, and an adventurous mind."

—David Dye, President, Dye Leadership Consulting

Wild
LEADERSHIP

Wild
LEADERSHIP

—— ◆ ——

What Nature Teaches Us About Adaptability, Resilience, and Intuition

JOHN W. SIGMON

JONES MEDIA
PUBLISHING

Wild Leadership: What Nature Teaches Us About Adaptability, Resilience, and Intuition

Jones Media Publishing
10645 N. Tatum Blvd. Ste. 200-166
Phoenix, AZ 85028
JonesMediaPublishing.com

Disclaimer:

The author strives to be as accurate and complete as possible in the creation of this book, notwithstanding the fact that the author does not warrant or represent at any time that the contents within are accurate due to the rapidly changing nature of the Internet. While all attempts have been made to verify information provided in this publication, the Author and the Publisher assume no responsibility and are not liable for errors, omissions, or contrary interpretation of the subject matter herein. The Author and Publisher hereby disclaim any liability, loss or damage incurred as a result of the application and utilization, whether directly or indirectly, of any information, suggestion, advice, or procedure in this book. Any perceived slights of specific persons, peoples, or organizations are unintentional.

Printed in the United States of America

ISBN: 978-1-948382-95-3 paperback

Thank you for being a valued reader!

As a token of appreciation, you're invited to download
a nature inspired reflection guide. Allow the power of nature
guide your leadership reflections. , ignite your curiosity,
and fuel innovative thinking.

Get it here: WildLeadershipBook.com/reader-bonus-page

TABLE OF CONTENTS

FOREWORD

L eadership, in its truest form, calls for more than strategy and execution. It demands heart, wisdom, and purpose. In *Wild Leadership: What Nature Teaches Us About Adaptability, Resilience, and Intuition,* John W. Sigmon offers an extraordinary exploration of these essential qualities. Drawing on his deep connection to the natural world and decades of experience guiding leaders, John masterfully bridges the wild and the workplace. He reveals how the timeless principles of nature can inspire leadership that is not only adaptable and resilient but also deeply intuitive.

In a world that often prizes urgency over reflection, *Wild Leadership* serves as a refreshing call to rethink how we lead. Through vivid storytelling—whether describing the quiet persistence of bamboo, the strength of a salmon swimming upstream, or the intuitive harmony of a flock of birds—John illuminates how nature provides a blueprint for leading with clarity and courage, even in the face of uncertainty.

What sets this book apart is its unique blend of inspiration and action. John doesn't merely share insights; he equips readers with practical exercises that encourage them to not just think differently but to act with renewed purpose. His work challenges us to pause, observe, and draw wisdom from the natural rhythms and patterns that have endured for millennia.

For anyone feeling overwhelmed by the pressures of modern leadership or seeking to reconnect with their inner compass, *Wild Leadership* offers a path forward. It is a guide not only to professional success but also to personal growth. John's wisdom, honesty, and thoughtful guidance transform this book into more than a manual—it is a companion for the journey of becoming a leader who embraces both the wildness of the world and the leader within.

Reading *Wild Leadership* feels like a conversation with a trusted mentor, one who reminds you that the greatest lessons in leadership can often be found by stepping outside and looking to the natural world. As you turn these pages, prepare to be inspired, challenged, and equipped to lead with greater clarity, resilience, and authenticity.

Payal Jindal Khanna is a trailblazer in leadership coaching, known for her groundbreaking work at Shoolini University, where she fosters a culture of empowerment and compassion. A recipient of the prestigious ICF India Coaching Conclave Trailblazer Excellence Coach Award and a passionate advocate for authentic connections, her work bridges global best practices with transformative education. Drawing from the teachings of Tsunesaburo Makiguchi, Payal's philosophy of leadership and coaching centers on empathy, inclusivity, and the pursuit of meaningful growth, making her an ideal voice for this foreword

INTRODUCTION

I had a challenging childhood. My parents were teenagers when I was born, trying to figure out their own lives while raising me. They leaned heavily on my grandparents, who lived nearby. I spent most weekends and many summers in their care. Nature was an important part of their lives and, as a result, mine. I spent many hours exploring the gardens of my grandparents' home. We'd wander through fields of wildflowers, and they shared their joy of the land and its inhabitants. I hung onto every word. They instilled in me a deep reverence for the natural world, a love for its rhythms and cycles, and an appreciation for its boundless wisdom.

On weekends, we'd often journey to their property in the North Carolina mountains, about a three-hour drive. On the property was a pop-up camper at the bottom of a steep slope. At the top of the hill, we could see across the border to the Tennessee range of the Smoky Mountains. My grandfather, a man of quiet strength and resilience, often hiked with me through the nearby woods. As we walked, he'd point out the intricate details of the forest— the patterns of a spider's web, a moss-covered rock, or a natural spring. He taught me to see the world through curiosity and wonder, appreciate the interconnectedness of all living things, and find inspiration in nature's resilience and adaptability.

My grandmother, a woman of boundless intuition, shared her deep connection to the natural world. She had an uncanny ability to sense subtle shifts in weather, the changing seasons, and the needs of the plants and animals around her. She taught me to listen to my intuition, to trust my gut feelings, and to find guidance in the intelligence of nature.

As I grew older, I carried these lessons into my professional life. I became a leader, navigating the complexities of work and life. I often relied on the wisdom and insights I gleaned from nature and my grandparents. I learned that the most influential leaders can adapt to change, embrace uncertainty, and trust their intuition. They are the ones who can inspire their teams to collaborate, innovate, and persevere in the face of challenges.

Yet, as I climbed the corporate ladder, I noticed a disturbing trend. Many of us had lost touch with the natural world. We spent our days confined to sterile office buildings, our minds consumed by work demands. We needed to remember the simple joys of spending time in nature, the restorative power of connecting with the earth, and the valuable lessons the natural world can teach us about leadership and life.

I invite you to rediscover the wisdom of the wild. We will explore the profound connection between nature and leadership through stories, reflections, and practical exercises. We will learn how to harness nature's power to cultivate adaptability, resilience, and intuition—the essential qualities of effective leadership. We will discover how to reconnect with the natural world, find inspiration in its beauty and wisdom, and bring its lessons back into our workplaces and lives.

The wild offers us a path to renewal and growth in a chaotic and disconnected world. Nature is a source of inspiration, a teacher, and a reminder of our interconnectedness with all living things. By embracing the wild, we can become better leaders, colleagues, and human beings.

Each section of this book—Adaptability, Resilience, and Intuition—is explored through the lens of nature, offering practical guidance and suggestions to help you delve deeper and expand your understanding. The examples and metaphors I share, drawn from nature, reflect what inspires me. I encourage you to look to the natural world around you, discover what moves you, and let it guide your journey of growth and discovery.

ADAPTABILITY

"Adaptability is about the powerful difference between adapting to cope and adapting to win."

—Max McKeown

Nature Finds a Way

CHAPTER 1

CLARITY, COMMUNICATION, AND TEAMWORK

ike many other boys my age, I was curious about the stereotypical "creepy, crawly" things: spiders, frogs, and the like. When I was eight, I joined the local Scout Troop like many kids in my rural community. It was an adventure I loved—camping, crafting, and soaking up everything I could about nature.

At the time, the Scouts published a magazine called Boy's Life (now Scout Life), and I eagerly flipped through every issue. The back pages were packed with ads for all kinds of kid treasures: x-ray glasses, pet chameleons, pocket knives—and one ad that stopped me in my tracks: an ant farm.

The ad was simple: a black-and-white sketch of a clear plastic case on a little stand. Tiny ants worked hard, creating an intricate web of tunnels and chambers. It looked like a miniature world full of life and energy, and I couldn't stop thinking about it.

For no reason other than thinking it was the coolest thing ever, I nervously asked my parents if I could spend my allowance and savings on that ant farm. After a bit of back-and-forth (and some pleading), they finally said yes.

In 1968, buying something wasn't as easy as a quick click. You had to fill out an order form by hand, write a check, and mail it to the vendor. Then you waited—patiently—for weeks. Times have changed, and we've all adapted to a new way of doing things, but there was something special about that old-school process.

Organizations, communities, and families face unprecedented challenges that demand agility, clarity, and effective communication. The ant colony offers lessons in leadership and adaptability with a highly organized system where each member plays a vital role in achieving the collective goal. The behaviors and structures within an ant colony offer insights into adaptability, organizational clarity, and teamwork—crucial elements for effective leadership.

One of the most striking aspects of an ant colony is the meticulous division of labor. The exact nature of labor division reminds us of the importance of organizational clarity. Clarity is crucial for any team or structure. Still, it becomes even more essential in matrixed organizations, where complexity can easily lead to confusion. Each ant has a distinct role in ensuring tasks are executed efficiently. Productively, organizations thrive when roles, responsibilities, and goals are clearly defined.

At the heart of this clarity lies the organization's ability to consistently evaluate its operations and direction through the lens of its core values and overarching vision. This alignment not only minimizes confusion but also maximizes focus and effectiveness, creating a shared purpose that drives everyone forward.

The ant colony shares information transparently via pheromone trails. These chemical markers convey vital information to the entire colony, signaling births, deaths, or the discovery of food sources. While humans don't rely on pheromones, we can take inspiration from the ants' seamless flow of information.

This highlights the importance of multimodal communication for leaders—using diverse and effective methods to ensure messages are clear and impactful. The ant's pheromone trail challenges us to reflect on how we communicate: Are we capturing attention? Are we inspiring action? By embracing consistent and engaging communication, we can foster alignment and collaboration as effortlessly as an ant colony navigating its world.

Promoting and driving organizational clarity can sometimes feel contradictory. For instance, the ant colony has a well-defined and communicated hierarchy, facilitating efficient decision-making and resource allocation. Similarly, our organizations have clear hierarchies, yet leadership is also shared among members, contributing to the overall adaptability. Embracing organizational clarity alongside a distributed leadership model can set an organization apart. Too often, we fall into the trap of "either-or thinking," but more often than not, we're better served by adopting "and thinking."

Take organizational structure as an example: choosing between a clear hierarchy with defined roles and responsibilities or a matrixed organization with self-directed work teams is not a matter. We can have both. By blending the two approaches and leaning into the power of teamwork and collaboration, organizations can create a structure that fosters clarity while empowering flexibility and innovation. It's about finding the best balance for your team and vision.

The extraordinary success of an ant colony exemplifies the power of teamwork and collaboration. The colony's achievements build upon the collective effort of its members. Each ant contributes to the common goals, from food foraging and nurturing the young to defending the nest. This unified effort underscores the power of teamwork. In an organizational context, teamwork is indispensable for achieving complex goals. Leaders must foster a collaborative environment where employees work together harmoniously toward a shared goal. Leaders can spark innovation and boost adaptability by tapping into each team member's unique skills and perspectives.

In navigating organizational clarity, hierarchy, communication, strategic alignment, and teamwork are inseparable. Each ant in the colony understands its role, and their efforts harmonize to create cohesion. This is the essence of strategic alignment, where shared purpose and individual contributions are inseparable. Effective teamwork brings this vision to life as individuals communicate, cooperate, and coordinate their efforts toward a common goal. With trust as their foundation, teams embrace the organization's vision, commit to shared goals, and navigate the complexities of change with resilience and adaptability. In this narrative of trust, alignment, and teamwork, the true potential of any organization unfolds, with its members united in a shared pursuit of excellence.

Organizational clarity serves as a guiding light for adaptability, much like an unobstructed vision and purpose direct the actions of an ant colony. The goal of survival and reproduction drives all activities, ensuring alignment among all members. In organizations, a compelling vision and purpose are essential for navigating change. Leaders must articulate a vision that inspires and motivates teams, offering direction and clarity on how individual efforts contribute to the larger goals. When employees resonate with the organization's purpose, they are more likely to embrace change, be more engaged, and contribute to its adaptability.

The lessons from my childhood ant farm have stayed with me throughout my career. In every team I've been part of or had the privilege to lead, I've seen how clarity, seamless communication, and collaboration are the lifeblood of success.

Ants continually remind me of the transformative power of organizational clarity, teamwork, and effective communication. As leaders, we can nurture these qualities within our organizations—creating spaces where people feel empowered, informed, and united around a common purpose. By embracing the wisdom of the ant colony, we can navigate the complexities of modern organizations with greater skill, building resilient, adaptable teams that survive and thrive in the face of change.

Leadership Reflections:

1. **What steps can I take to ensure roles and responsibilities within my team are clearly defined and understood?**

   - Schedule regular meetings to discuss and review team roles, ensuring everyone understands their responsibilities and how their role contributes to the broader goals.

   - Document and share a clear outline of roles and expectations, ensuring responsibilities are easily accessible to all team members.

   - Encourage open dialogue, allowing team members to ask questions or seek clarification on any aspects of their role. This will ensure alignment and reduce confusion.

2. **What communication channels will ensure a seamless and transparent information flow?**

   - Leverage a mix of communication tools—such as team messaging apps, regular check-ins, and collaborative platforms—to ensure everyone can access the information they need.

- Establish communication best practices, such as regular updates and transparent sharing of key information, so everyone is on the same page.
- Create an open-door policy that encourages team members to voice concerns or share ideas, ensuring that communication flows freely in all directions.

3. **What strategies can I implement to foster a culture of trust within my team?**

- Lead by example, demonstrating honesty, transparency, and consistency in your actions and decisions.
- Encourage a collaborative environment where team members feel safe sharing ideas, asking for help, and offering constructive feedback without fear of judgment.
- Acknowledge and celebrate individual and team successes, reinforcing a culture of recognition and mutual respect.

Micro Actions:

- I will schedule a team meeting to review and clarify roles and responsibilities, ensuring everyone understands their contributions and how they align with the organization's broader goals.
- I will establish regular feedback loops to gather input from both my team and peers on the effectiveness of our communication, allowing us to identify areas for improvement.
- I will design a team-building activity that fosters collaboration and trust, encouraging a sense of shared responsibility and mutual support among team members.

CHAPTER 2

RESOURCEFULNESS AND INCLUSION

One winter, my brother and I traveled to Florida to watch our favorite football teams go head-to-head. It was a perfect February day in Miami, and with a few hours to spare before the game, we decided to visit Key Biscayne and Biscayne National Park. It was there that I first learned about the mangrove tree.

The mangrove tree thrives in coastal regions where the land meets the sea, often in swampy areas where fresh and saltwater mix. My introduction to the mangrove was unexpected. While walking along the beach, I dropped some papers, and the wind swept them away. As I hurried to collect them, I encountered a small group of strange-looking trees. Catching my breath from the dash, I ran into a park ranger. Overcome by curiosity, I asked him about the unusual trees. He explained they were mangrove trees and added that they were protected—damaging, destroying, or removing them was illegal. While he continued speaking, I lingered on his mention of preserving these unique trees. I made a mental note to learn more.

The mangrove's ability to thrive in harsh conditions stems from its mastery of resource optimization. The environments where mangroves thrive require them to maximize limited resources, a lesson that translates into leadership. Mangroves exhibit a keen sense of resource allocation. Their roots, submerged in salty water, filter out salt, allowing the tree to access fresh water. This selective process ensures the tree gets what it needs to survive in a resource-scarce environment.

Similarly, influential leaders must excel at resource allocation, providing their teams with the necessary skills, physical resources, and opportunities to thrive while navigating constraints. Leaders must also be adept at separating the "signal from the noise," like the mangrove separates the salt from the water. The mangrove's ability to flourish in challenging conditions comes from its mastery of resource allocation, innovation, and sustainability—principles that seamlessly translate into effective leadership.

Leaders, like the mangrove's roots, must carefully distribute resources to ensure their teams thrive, even under constraints. I work with many startup CEOs who face limited capital, and they often mirror the mangrove's ability to prioritize and filter resources. These CEOs focus on areas with the highest potential return, sometimes directing funds toward product development and marketing while being more cautious with administrative expenses. By being selective and strategic, they ensure their teams can grow and adapt, even when resources are scarce.

Resource allocation involves strategic human capital, technology, and infrastructure decisions in more established organizations. Leaders may need to reallocate resources from underperforming projects or prioritize employee development to build a skilled workforce. The key is to align resource allocation with organizational goals, maximizing impact and supporting long-term success.

Beyond careful resource allocation, the mangrove's complex root system creates a firm anchoring while creating a vibrant ecosystem. Similarly, leaders can foster innovation within their organizations. During a recent visit to a manufacturing facility facing raw material shortages due to global supply chain challenges, the leadership team explored alternative materials and methods, including using generative artificial intelligence to help solve the challenge of finding alternative chemical compounds. The mindset of creativity and adaptability allowed the organization to function effectively even when traditional resources were scarce.

Leaders can encourage their teams to streamline processes, leverage technology, and expand their skill sets. By promoting continuous improvement and resourcefulness, leaders create an environment where innovation thrives, and the organization stays agile.

Beyond fostering innovation, mangroves create a sustainable ecosystem by enriching the soil and preventing erosion. Leaders can emulate this by prioritizing long-term success over short-term gains. Investing in employee development and well-being fosters a stable and productive work environment, leading to sustained organizational success.

Sustainability requires considering both the environmental and social impact of the organization's actions. Leaders can adopt eco-friendly practices, support community initiatives, and promote ethical conduct to enhance sustainability. This integrated approach enhances the organization's brand reputation and long-term viability and contributes to a better world.

The mangrove's resilience in harsh conditions provides valuable insights that leaders can apply as they navigate their challenges. By mastering resource allocation, fostering innovation, and embracing sustainability, leaders can effectively navigate constraints, drive growth, and ensure their organizations thrive in an ever-changing world.

Effective leadership requires strength and adaptability to navigate complexity and uncertainty. Mangroves have a complex system of roots that allow them to remain grounded despite shifting tides and storms. In turbulent times, leaders, anchored in their core values, have a built-in guide for their decisions and actions. Core values serve as a compass, helping leaders navigate ethical dilemmas and make decisions aligned with the organization's purpose and mission. Core values also create a sense of stability and predictability, which is particularly important during uncertainty and change. By staying true to their core values, leaders inspire confidence and loyalty within their teams, fostering a culture of trust and accountability.

While mangroves are firmly rooted, their branches and leaves are flexible, allowing them to bend with the wind rather than break. This flexibility is essential for leaders who adapt their strategies to changing circumstances and maintain their core mission. Consider the many retail companies that must adapt to market shifts and technological advancements. Leaders with rooted flexibility adapt by integrating modern technologies into their business model while maintaining a commitment to customer satisfaction. This ability to pivot while keeping a clear vision ensures the organization's continued relevance and success.

Adaptability also demands a willingness to learn and experiment. Leaders must be open to the latest ideas, embrace feedback, and be ready to adjust their course when necessary. Being open to new ideas means staying within core values and mission but finding creative ways to achieve them in a changing landscape.

Leaders must show resilience in adversity, inspiring their teams to persevere. I accompanied a leadership team during a recent financial downturn as they prepared to address their teams. Despite their concerns, their ability to adapt to the moment's needs and communicate transparently with their team provided support and fostered a sense of unity. Even though the news was not pleasant to deliver or hear, the leaders created an environment where they could collectively navigate their financial challenges and emerge stronger. By modeling a positive attitude, staying anchored to their values, and a willingness to learn, leaders create a culture of adaptability where setbacks are stepping stones to success.

As mangroves contribute to their ecosystems, influential leaders build solid organizational ecosystems, creating a culture of collaboration, fostering diversity, and nurturing talent. Mangroves provide a habitat for a wide variety of species, fostering an ecosystem where each organism plays a role in maintaining balance. Similarly, leaders should promote collaboration and inclusion within their organizations, recognizing that diverse perspectives and skills contribute to overall success. A leader might form cross-functional teams to tackle complex projects, encouraging open communication and cooperation.

By valuing collaboration, leaders harness their team's strengths, leading to innovative solutions and enhanced performance. Collaboration can be fostered through various methods, such as creating opportunities for team members to interact and share ideas, providing tools for collaboration, and recognizing and rewarding collaborative efforts. Leaders can also model collaborative behavior by seeking input from their team, valuing diverse perspectives, and creating an environment where everyone feels comfortable contributing their ideas.

Mangroves illustrate the importance of diversity in creating a robust ecosystem. Leaders can learn from this by fostering diversity and inclusion within their teams, recognizing that varied backgrounds and experiences enrich the organization. By creating an inclusive environment where everyone feels valued, leaders ensure that the organization benefits from various ideas and perspectives, driving innovation and growth.

Diversity and inclusion involve more than just hiring people from diverse backgrounds. It's about creating a culture where everyone feels safe expressing their opinions, contributing ideas, and being authentic. Leaders can foster this culture by promoting open dialogue, addressing unconscious biases, and creating opportunities for everyone to participate and contribute.

Just as mangroves nurture their environment, contributing to its health and sustainability, leaders should focus on nurturing their teams. This includes fostering talent development by providing mentorship programs, continuous learning opportunities, and clear paths for career progression to ensure team members have the support and resources they need to grow and succeed.

Leaders must build a robust and capable workforce that drives the organization forward by investing in their team's development. Talent development is an ongoing process that requires commitment from both leaders and employees. Leaders can support team growth by providing regular and specific feedback, offering challenging assignments, and creating a culture of learning and development. Leaders enhance individual performance by investing in their team's potential and creating a more engaged, motivated workforce.

Leadership Reflections:

1. **What is my definition of optimizing resource allocation?**
   - Strategically directing available resources—time, capital, or talent—toward areas that deliver the greatest impact and value.
   - Focusing on efficiency and long-term goals while remaining flexible to adapt to changing circumstances.

2. **What steps can I take to build resilience and adaptability while staying grounded in my core values?**
   - Invest in developing problem-solving skills within the team.
   - Encourage learning from challenges and setbacks.
   - Maintain clear, consistent communication to keep everyone aligned.
   - Reinforce core values in team discussions, decision-making, and strategies to ensure adaptability aligns with our stand.

3. **What practices can I adopt to foster a culture of innovation and sustainability, even in challenging conditions?**
   - Create an environment that encourages experimentation and embraces failure as a learning opportunity.
   - Support continuous improvement through recognition and rewarding creative solutions.
   - Foster cross-functional collaboration to promote diverse ideas.
   - Prioritize sustainability in both environmental and operational terms to ensure long-term innovation.

Micro Actions:

- I will conduct a detailed review of my team's resources and identify areas for optimization, ensuring we are directing our efforts in the most effective ways possible.
- Initiate or enhance programs that develop resilience within my team, providing them with tools, mentorship, and opportunities to build adaptability in their work and mindset.
- I will implement practices that promote long-term sustainability within my organization by encouraging eco-friendly initiatives, supporting community outreach, and investing in employee development to foster growth and innovation.

CHAPTER 3

FACING ADVERSITY

My grandparents felt a deep connection to everything native, including people. Though my grandmother lacked formal education, her passions more than made up for it. She was an avid reader and lifelong learner. One of her greatest interests was studying indigenous peoples. I always sensed her curiosity about them was personal, though I lacked the wisdom and courage to ask her directly as a child. However, my grandmother was a generous storyteller, especially regarding animals. She often shared tales of how different animal species adapted to their environments, drawing from the books she read about the relationships between indigenous populations and animals. One of her favorite stories was about a family of foxes that had taken shelter under the porch of her rustic cabin. Her storytelling ability was nothing short of magical. Through her stories about animals and nature, she would highlight how they adapted and thrived in even the harshest environments. The Arctic fox, for example, became one of her most beloved examples of resilience and adaptation.

The Arctic fox symbolizes perseverance and adaptability. Imagine thriving in a climate where temperatures regularly range from 0 to 20°F. By studying the fox's mental toughness, resourcefulness, and proactive risk management, we can glean valuable lessons for today's and tomorrow's leadership challenges. These insights can help leaders cultivate resilience, foster innovation, and anticipate challenges in their roles and organizations.

The Arctic fox's ability to survive in one of the harshest environments on Earth is a powerful testament to its extraordinary mental toughness. Facing bitter cold, unrelenting winds, and nearly constant snow, the Arctic is a place where survival demands physical endurance and mental resilience. The fox's endurance under these extreme conditions serves as a reminder of how essential mental fortitude is in overcoming adversity and thriving in the face of hardship. This resilience isn't just about surviving—it's about persevering and finding ways to adapt, even when the odds seem insurmountable.

During the prolonged Arctic winters, the Arctic fox exemplifies remarkable composure with minimal daylight and scarce food. It does not succumb to panic or despair; instead, it relies on its instincts and deep understanding of the environment to navigate challenges. The fox's ability to remain calm under pressure is critical for its survival, allowing it to make calculated decisions in a high-stress environment.

Like the Arctic fox, leaders must cultivate mental toughness to navigate demanding roles. Mental resilience enables leaders to handle stress, stay focused on objectives, and persist despite setbacks. Developing mental toughness means embracing a growth mindset and viewing challenges as opportunities for learning and improvement rather than obstacles. It requires maintaining a steady demeanor, even when facing uncertainty or adversity, and leading by example to inspire confidence and stability within a team.

During a particularly turbulent period for a regional health insurer, I had the opportunity to work closely with the leadership team during a challenging transition. The CEO unexpectedly retired, and soon after, the Chief HR Officer (CHRO) followed suit. The Board quickly asked a senior member of the HR team to step in as the interim CHRO, taking on both the responsibilities of her current role and the added task of leading the recruiting efforts for a new CEO and CHRO.

As I worked alongside this team, it became clear that the interim leader's mental toughness was contagious. She remained focused on the positives while being realistic and transparent about the team's challenges. By openly demonstrating vulnerability and maintaining mental toughness, she fostered a sense of stability and trust within the organization. Her leadership empowered the team to embrace a growth mindset and prioritize well-being for themselves and their colleagues.

Ultimately, this resilience paid off. The interim leader successfully navigated the turbulence and became the new CHRO, with a new CEO recruited in record time. Today, the organization continues to thrive, adding significant value to its stakeholders—proof that with the right leadership and mental resilience, even the most difficult transitions can lead to lasting success.

Leaders who embody the Arctic fox's persistence, mental toughness, and adaptability are better equipped to guide their teams through turbulent times. By fostering a culture of resilience, leaders can empower their teams to persevere through difficulties and emerge stronger. Building a culture of resilience involves helping team members develop their resilience skills, providing resources for stress management, and cultivating an environment where challenges meet determination and creativity.

Resourcefulness is a defining trait of the Arctic fox, essential for survival in a resource-constrained environment. Like the mangrove tree, the Arctic fox displays exceptional ingenuity and adaptability in a harsh environment where food is scarce. Its white winter coat serves as camouflage against the snowy backdrop and as a means to conserve heat. This adaptation allows the fox to blend seamlessly into its environment, enhancing its ability to hunt and evade predators.

The Arctic fox's ability to adapt its coat color as the seasons change is a remarkable example of nature's ingenuity. Its thick white coat blends seamlessly with the snow in winter, providing perfect camouflage against predators and prey alike. But as the snow melts and the landscape transforms into rocky, tundra terrain, the fox's coat changes to brown or gray, allowing it to maintain its stealth and effectiveness in a new environment. This seasonal shift reflects the fox's resourcefulness and adaptability, demonstrating its keen awareness of shifting conditions and ability to adjust its strategy to ensure survival.

The Arctic fox's resourcefulness goes beyond its physical adaptations; its hunting techniques are another prime example of how it makes the most of its environment. Whether leaping to detect prey beneath the snow, using its sharp smell to locate buried carcasses, or scavenging leftovers from polar bears, the fox shows that resourcefulness is not just about using what's immediately available but creatively navigating challenges to secure what's needed. In times of scarcity, the fox's ability to adapt and strategize ensures it can find food, even when conditions are less than ideal.

For leaders, this mindset is crucial in today's ever-changing business world. Just as the Arctic fox adjusts its hunting strategies to overcome challenges, leaders must leverage available resources creatively and innovatively. Encouraging teams to think outside the box, experiment with new approaches, and use existing resources effectively empowers them to overcome obstacles and seize opportunities, even in difficult circumstances. A culture of resourcefulness within an organization fosters resilience, adaptability, and the ability to thrive in the face of scarcity or uncertainty.

Leaders who embrace resourcefulness as a core value are better positioned to guide their teams through change, drive innovation, and ensure that their organization is agile and prepared for future challenges. By freeing up intellectual capital and empowering teams to maximize available resources, these leaders can create a more sustainable, adaptable, and successful organization in the long run.

Resourcefulness also entails continuous learning and improvement. Just as the Arctic fox adapts its strategies to environmental changes, leaders must stay informed about industry trends and emerging technologies. Look beyond your current industry. *How can you learn from how other industries are approaching a given situation?* Leaders can drive innovation and maintain a competitive edge by staying agile and open to new ideas. Innovative leaders create an environment where experimentation is encouraged, and failures are viewed as opportunities for growth and learning. Of course, this does not happen by magic. Leaders, like the Arctic fox, must be proactive and intentional in their approach. It is not enough to simply say, "We have to think outside the box." The most impactful leaders create a structure or a framework for experimentation that is widely understood and almost universally includes a way to measure success and mitigate risk.

Proactivity is indeed a cornerstone of the Arctic fox's survival strategy. In the extreme conditions of the Arctic, where survival hinges on anticipating and managing risks, the fox demonstrates an exceptional ability to stay vigilant and plan. Its proactive behavior is visible in its constantly scanning the environment for potential threats, adjusting its movements to avoid danger, and taking preventive measures when necessary. For example, the fox knows when to hunker down in its den during severe storms or shift its hunting strategy depending on changing weather patterns or the presence of predators.

This proactive mindset is critical for leaders in navigating uncertainty and mitigating potential risks. Just as the Arctic fox is constantly attuned to its environment, leaders must remain aware of the shifting dynamics in their organizations, industries, and broader markets. Proactive leaders anticipate challenges before they arise, taking strategic actions to minimize risks and protect their teams. Whether anticipating market shifts, planning for potential disruptions, or fostering a culture of preparedness, proactivity allows leaders to maintain control and steer their organizations through turbulent times.

Proactivity also means inviting a culture of strategic foresight within teams. Leaders should encourage team members to anticipate challenges and proactively seek solutions. They should promote a proactive mindset where individuals are empowered to identify and address potential issues before they become significant problems. Leaders can effectively enhance their teams' ability to respond to emerging challenges by instilling ownership and accountability. Leaders who exhibit proactivity are better equipped to guide their teams through change and uncertainty, keeping them focused and resilient in achieving their goals.

With its mental toughness, resourcefulness, and proactivity, the Arctic fox is an inspiring model for contemporary leadership. Its ability to thrive in one of the Earth's harshest environments provides valuable lessons for leaders in various sectors. The Arctic fox's lessons provide valuable insights for leadership:

- **Mental Toughness:** The Arctic fox's ability to endure extreme conditions exemplifies the importance of mental toughness. Leaders who cultivate resilience can maintain composure during tough situations, inspiring their teams to do the same. They foster an environment where challenges are met with determination, ensuring teams remain focused and confident in navigating adversity.

- **Resourcefulness:** The Arctic fox's adaptability in utilizing various hunting techniques and adjusting to seasonal changes highlights the need for resourcefulness in leadership. In an ever-changing business landscape, leaders must creatively leverage available resources and remain flexible. By encouraging innovation and resourcefulness, leaders can ensure their teams are equipped to tackle challenges and capitalize on opportunities.

These principles—mental toughness and resourcefulness—are crucial for fostering a culture of resilience and adaptability within teams. Leaders who embody these traits can guide their organizations through uncertainty, creating pathways for long-term success.

Proactivity, as shown by the Arctic fox's strategic risk management, highlights the importance of foresight and planning in leadership. Proactive leaders anticipate challenges, develop contingency plans, and take preemptive actions to safeguard their organizations. By fostering a proactive mindset within their teams, leaders improve their ability to navigate uncertainties and achieve long-term success.

The Arctic fox symbolizes resilience, adaptability, and innovation in adversity. Its ability to thrive in one of the Earth's most challenging environments inspires leaders in all sectors. By emulating the Arctic fox's traits, leaders can navigate the complexities of the modern world, overcome challenges, and achieve success through perseverance, creativity, and strategic foresight. Leaders can build resilient and successful organizations by applying the lessons of the Arctic fox, fostering a brighter and more sustainable future for themselves and future generations.

Leadership Reflections:

1. **What is my response under pressure?**
   - Do I remain calm and focused, or do I feel overwhelmed and reactive?
   - How can I improve my stress management techniques to maintain clarity during challenging situations?
   - How do I communicate under pressure to ensure my team remains confident and aligned?

2. **What new ideas and approaches am I open to?**
   - Am I regularly seeking feedback from my team to gain new perspectives?
   - How can I foster a culture that encourages experimentation and embraces new ideas?
   - What are some specific areas in my leadership or organization where I could try different approaches to improve results?

3. **What proactive steps can I take to identify potential risks and vulnerabilities within my organization?**

   - How can I implement regular risk assessments and scenario planning sessions with my team?
   - What tools or frameworks can I use to monitor changes in the market, industry, or internal operations?
   - How can I build stronger communication channels to surface potential risks early in the process?

Micro Actions:

   - I will spend a few minutes daily on mindfulness meditation, deep breathing, or an alternative reflective practice to cultivate calmness and focus.
   - I regularly engage with people from diverse backgrounds and viewpoints to broaden my understanding and challenge my assumptions.
   - I will conduct "what-if" exercises with my team to explore potential challenges and develop contingency plans.

RESILIENCE

"The oak fought the wind and was broken, the willow bent when it must and survived."

—Robert Jordan

Resilience Abounds in Nature

CHAPTER 4

RESILIENCE

Gardening is a passion of mine, and it brings me a deep sense of satisfaction to care for the gardens around my home. From planting vibrant flowers in the spring to garlic in the autumn, gardening is not just a hobby—it's a meditative practice that helps me find balance and peace. When I purchased my first home in a densely populated neighborhood, I wanted to create privacy with a natural fence or hedge. In my quest for the perfect solution, I stumbled upon an article that praised bamboo for its ability to spread easily and form an excellent sound barrier. Excited by the prospect, I didn't take the time to finish reading the article— a mistake I'd soon regret!

I found a nursery that sold bamboo plants, and the master gardener there jokingly warned me, "That bamboo will take over your yard." He recommended installing a barrier to contain its spread. I pictured a whimsical scene of bamboo gracefully waltzing across the lawn as he spoke. I almost told him that spreading was exactly what I wanted, but I didn't fully understand what lay ahead.

New shoots began to appear a few months later, stretching their delicate tips toward the sun. They grew at an astonishing pace, sometimes inches in a single day. The bamboo's relentless drive to expand became both amusing and frustrating. One morning, I found a rogue shoot pushing through a crack in the foundation of my garden shed! Even through concrete, the bamboo's unstoppable growth became a metaphor for life's challenges and resilience. However, it also became a point of contention with my neighbors as the shoots began to spread into their yards.

Bamboo has an unassuming presence that conceals its strength and resilience, characteristics of its deep-rooted patience and consistency. Bamboo isn't a plant for the impatient. Its most remarkable growth occurs beneath the surface, where a vast network of roots establishes a foundation for future strength. Much like the mangrove tree, the bamboo plant is grounded in a profound system of roots. This hidden growth can take years, during which the bamboo seems dormant. Yet beneath the soil, it builds a robust system that supports its rapid ascent. Similarly, leadership is about more than instant gratification or overnight success. It involves laying a solid foundation, nurturing potential, and fostering a resilient culture.

Building a successful team or organization is like cultivating a thriving bamboo forest. It demands time, dedication, unwavering commitment, and attentiveness. Successful leadership nurtures talent, fosters a positive culture, and consistently progresses toward goals. Like the bamboo's hidden growth, these efforts may not be immediately visible, but they are essential for long-term success.

Leaders who lack patience may feel discouraged by slow progress or be tempted to take shortcuts. The constant pressure to deliver results, meet quarterly targets or outperform competitors can lead to a focus on short-term gains, jeopardizing long-term sustainability. The bamboo is a potent reminder that true resilience comes from staying the course, even when results are not immediately apparent. Leaders create a solid foundation for future growth and success by consistently investing in their teams and organizations. This investment can include mentorship programs, continuous learning opportunities, or fostering an environment where open communication and constructive feedback are encouraged.

Warren Buffett is the Chairman and CEO of Berkshire Hathaway and one of the best-known investors in the world. His primary investment philosophy is patience and long-term thinking. He famously said, "The stock market is a device for transferring money from the impatient to the patient." This patience and long-term view have benefited him, as his company, Berkshire Hathaway, consistently outperforms the market over the long term. Buffett's success underscores the importance of resisting the allure of quick wins in favor of sustainable growth. It reminds us that the most impactful leadership decisions often require patience, nurturing, and trust.

Bamboo's resilience is rooted in its unseen strength and remarkable flexibility. Its hollow stalks allow it to bend and sway in the wind without breaking, which is critical for surviving storms and high winds. While rigid trees may snap under pressure, bamboo's openness helps it weather adversity and emerge stronger.

Adapting is not just desirable; it's essential. Technological advancements, shifting market dynamics, and unforeseen crises reshape business minute by minute—leaders who cling to outdated methods or resist new ideas risk putting their careers and organizations at risk. The bamboo's graceful sway serves as a reminder that resilience comes from embracing change, not resisting it. In the face of shifting market trends, disruptive technologies, or unexpected crises, leaders must pivot, re-evaluate strategies, and chart new courses.

Embracing change requires listening to diverse perspectives, experimenting with new approaches, and learning from failures. It involves creating a culture that encourages curiosity, welcomes questions, and values diverse viewpoints. By cultivating a culture of adaptability, leaders foster an environment where innovation thrives and resilience flourishes. David M. Walker is an exemplary leader in this spirit. When Walker took over as Comptroller General of the US at the Government Accountability Office (GAO) in 1998, the GAO desperately needed revitalization.

Walker initiated a significant transformation, adopting a human capital strategy that became a model for the public sector. His bold moves in revitalizing the GAO workforce through flexible benefit offerings for employees, including a hybrid and remote work strategy, established GAO as a leader in government innovation long before remote/hybrid work became mainstream. Walker's leadership exemplifies the power of embracing change and recognizing that past successes may not suffice for the future. It underscores the importance of courageously challenging the status quo and pursuing new paths, even when they entail uncertainty and risk.

Adaptability implies continuous growth. Just as bamboo grows continuously after reaching its full height, producing new shoots, and expanding its roots, effective leadership is a journey of perpetual growth. Bamboo's continuous growth reminds us that leadership is not about reaching a destination but ongoing evolution and self-improvement.

Leaders embodying bamboo's spirit of continuous growth are committed to lifelong learning and development. They understand that there is always room for personal and professional improvement. They actively seek new knowledge, embrace feedback, and strive to enhance their skills. This commitment to growth stems from curiosity, a hunger for learning, and the recognition that the world is ever-changing and requires constant adaptation.

This dedication to growth benefits not only individual leaders but also their organizations. By fostering a culture of continuous learning, leaders empower employees to develop their talents and contribute to the organization's success, strengthening its overall resilience and adaptability. It creates a workforce that is agile, innovative, and capable of navigating modern complexities. When leaders prioritize their growth and encourage their teams to do the same, they create a virtuous cycle where learning becomes a core value, driving innovation and keeping the organization at the forefront of its industry.

Bamboo is a powerful metaphor for leadership resilience, with its unwavering growth, flexibility, and adaptability. Leaders can cultivate the qualities that bamboo exemplifies to build teams and organizations that survive and thrive amidst adversity. Bamboo's lessons are theoretical concepts and practical principles applicable in the real world. By reflecting on these lessons and taking concrete actions, leaders can foster a culture of resilience within their organizations, empowering teams to navigate challenges confidently and emerge stronger.

Leadership Reflections:

1. **What practices can I implement to foster a culture of patience and consistency within my team?**
   - Encourage long-term thinking by setting clear, achievable goals with milestones.
   - Promote a focus on progress over perfection, helping the team see the value in steady growth.

- Recognize and celebrate consistent effort and improvements, not just big wins.
- Lead by example, demonstrating patience during challenging times and remaining calm under pressure.

2. What steps can I take to create an environment that tolerates, actively encourages, and celebrates openness to change, fostering innovation and adaptability?

- Cultivate a "fail-forward" culture where mistakes are seen as learning opportunities.
- Provide platforms for team members to share new ideas and experiment with innovative solutions.
- Create regular channels for feedback to assess and improve processes continuously.
- Highlight and reward teams or individuals who embrace change and adapt successfully to new challenges.

3. In what ways can I model continuous learning and development for my team?

- Commit to personal development by attending workshops, reading industry books, taking relevant courses, and sharing insights with the team.
- Encourage team members to pursue learning opportunities and support their professional growth.
- Schedule regular knowledge-sharing sessions where team members can teach each other.
- Reflection should be a regular part of the team's workflow, and past projects should be reviewed to extract lessons and areas for improvement.

Micro Actions:

- I will establish a system for regular feedback and reflection.
- I will encourage experimentation and risk-taking by dedicating time each quarter to innovation projects, providing resources for new ideas, and fostering a culture that embraces calculated risks and views failures as learning opportunities.

CHAPTER 5

AGAINST ALL ODDS

T he journey of the Pacific salmon is one of the most powerful examples of tenacity in nature. From a young age, I was fascinated by its story. I vividly recall watching my favorite show, Mutual of Omaha's Wild Kingdom, where the salmon's relentless determination to return to its birthplace to spawn captivated me. Their journey, full of formidable challenges, is a potent metaphor for the obstacles leaders must navigate.

The Pacific salmon's life cycle begins in the freshwater streams where they hatch. After spending years in the vast ocean, they instinctively return to these streams to spawn. Their path home is fraught with challenges: strong currents pushing them off course, predators threatening their survival, and even waterfalls they must leap over to continue upstream. Yet, despite these numerous obstacles, the salmon remain resolute, driven by an innate sense of purpose.

Leaders also must navigate complex landscapes—shifting markets, technological advancements, and changing workforce dynamics. Just as the salmon must adjust to unpredictable waters, leaders must also demonstrate resilience and adaptability. However, the critical lesson from the salmon is not just perseverance but *purpose-driven* perseverance. The journey back to their spawning grounds is not merely about survival; it is about ensuring the continuity of future generations.

For leaders, tenacity without direction can lead to burnout or missteps. Like the salmon's tenacity, leadership tenacity must be purpose-driven. As we explore tenacity in this chapter, consider how this intrinsic purpose fuels resilience, sustains momentum, and enables leaders to endure and thrive amid adversity. Just as the salmon's journey ends in the continuation of life, a leader's tenacity should culminate in organizational growth and the development of future leaders.

The salmon's journey is not one of blind persistence; it is a testament to calculated risk-taking and adaptability. They assess the currents, gauge the height of waterfalls, and time their leaps with precision. Navigating complex river systems, they rely on their innate sense of smell and magnetic orientation to return to their natal streams. This adaptability and resourcefulness in the face of adversity are powerful reminders for leaders that the ability to pivot, learn, and evolve is crucial in navigating complexity.

Leaders, too, face challenges that demand tenacity. Economic fluctuations, technological disruptions, global pandemics, and shifting market dynamics create turbulent waters for any organization. The resilience of the salmon serves as a powerful reminder that persistence and adaptability are essential to achieving ambitious goals. When faced with obstacles, we should ask ourselves: What can I learn from this challenge, and how can it enhance my leadership? By embracing difficulties as opportunities for growth, we can transform setbacks into stepping stones toward even greater success.

Just as the salmon navigates its path with unwavering determination, leaders must remain focused on their objectives, embrace change, and persist when the currents of opposition grow strong. The ability to pivot strategies, learn from failures, and maintain a positive outlook is crucial for navigating complex, unpredictable environments. Whether adapting to new technologies, evolving customer preferences, or responding to unexpected crises, leaders must be willing to learn, experiment, and iterate.

The salmon's journey also underscores the importance of calculated risk-taking in leadership. Influential leaders understand that progress often requires stepping outside their comfort zones and embracing the unknown. One of my favorite expressions is, "There is no learning in the comfort zone and no comfort in the learning zone." Learning can be uncomfortable! Effective leaders weigh the potential rewards against risks, gather information, and make informed decisions. They are unafraid to challenge the status quo, experiment with new approaches, and learn from successes and failures.

Beyond tenacity and adaptability, the salmon's journey embodies a profound purpose. Their trek is not solely about survival; it is about fulfilling a biological imperative to ensure the continuation of their species. This purpose propels their relentless determination, guiding them back to their birthplace, no matter the cost. For leaders, this translates into the critical importance of having a clear vision and purpose that fuels action and inspires teams.

Influential leaders possess a strong sense of "why" behind their work, whether creating innovative products, addressing pressing social issues, or positively impacting their community. This purpose serves as a compass, guiding decisions and actions even when the path ahead is uncertain or clouded by doubt. The salmon's instinctual drive is a potent reminder for leaders to align their actions with a higher purpose beyond personal gain or short-term profits.

Purpose-driven leadership often results in greater resilience, passion, and inspiration for the leader and their team. It becomes a rallying cry, uniting individuals around a shared goal and fostering meaning and belonging. When people understand how their work contributes to a larger purpose, they are more likely to go the extra mile, overcome challenges, and achieve extraordinary results.

At the culmination of their arduous journey, the salmon's story reaches a poignant climax in an act of profound selflessness. Upon reaching their natal stream, their bodies transformed and weakened by the rigors of their travels, they spawn, expending every ounce of energy to ensure the next generation's survival. Many salmon perish shortly after that, their bodies returning to the earth to nourish the ecosystem sustaining them. This ultimate act of sacrifice is a powerful reminder of the importance of selflessness in leadership.

Authentic leadership is not about self-aggrandizement or personal glory but serving a more significant cause. The salmon's sacrifice teaches us that effective leadership involves prioritizing the needs of others and the organization over our own. It consists of nurturing talent, empowering teams, and ensuring the long-term sustainability of the collective effort. Serving a purpose greater than self can require making difficult decisions, sacrificing personal time and resources, and prioritizing the needs over individual recognition.

Leaders prioritizing their team's well-being and the organization's success create a more positive and productive work environment. By focusing on the collective good, they can achieve far greater results than they could. Their legacy is not defined by personal achievements but by their lasting impact on others and the world around them.

Selfless leaders cultivate a culture of trust and loyalty. They invest in the development of their team members, providing the resources and support necessary for success. They recognize and reward contributions, fostering a sense of appreciation and belonging. By prioritizing the needs of others, they create a ripple effect of positive impact that extends far beyond their immediate influence.

The salmon's tenacious journey—driven by purpose and culminating in selflessness—embodies leadership principles that transcend the natural world. Their story offers timeless lessons that guide us through leadership challenges, reminding us that true success lies not only in reaching our destination but also in the journey itself and the impact we leave behind.

By embracing the wisdom of the salmon, we can navigate challenges with greater confidence and purpose, leaving a legacy that benefits our organizations and the broader world. We can embody their unwavering spirit, focus on a purpose greater than ourselves, and cultivate ultimate selflessness. In doing so, we lead with respect for the past, a clear vision for the future, and a commitment to the well-being of all.

As leaders, we strive for success and contribute to a cause larger than ourselves. By integrating the lessons of the salmon into our leadership practices, we can become agents of positive change, leaving a legacy that extends far beyond our lifetimes. Like the salmon, our leadership journeys may be fraught with challenges; yet, with determination, purpose, and selflessness, we can overcome any obstacle and reach our destination, inspiring those who follow.

As leaders, let's embrace these lessons and navigate our challenges with unwavering determination and a commitment to the greater good. In the spirit of the salmon, let our leadership serve as a source of nourishment and inspiration, ensuring a thriving future for generations.

Leadership Reflections:

1. **What challenges am I currently facing, and how can I leverage them as opportunities for growth and learning?**
   - Evaluate recent setbacks and identify key lessons that can drive personal development.
   - Embrace challenges as opportunities to experiment with new strategies and approaches.
   - Seek feedback from my team and peers to uncover blind spots and refine my leadership approach.

2. **What is the deeper "why" behind my leadership?**
   - Reflect on my core values and how they align with the goals I am working towards.
   - Consider the impact I want on others and the legacy I hope to leave.
   - Assess how my leadership serves the greater good of my organization and community.

3. **How can I create a culture of trust, empowerment, and appreciation within my team?**
   - Lead by example, demonstrating openness, vulnerability, and accountability in all my interactions.

- Provide opportunities for team members to contribute ideas, make decisions, and take ownership of projects.
- Regularly acknowledge individual and team achievements, fostering a culture of recognition and gratitude.

Micro Actions:

- I will embrace challenges by identifying one current obstacle and proactively seeking ways to learn and grow.
- I will communicate my purpose by scheduling a team meeting or one-on-one conversations to share my leadership vision.
- I will recognize contributions by consciously acknowledging and appreciating my team members' efforts, individually and collectively.

CHAPTER 6

THE CACTUS CODE

A small cactus sits at the heart of my workspace, surrounded by scattered notes and well-worn books. Though unassuming, this tiny desert dweller offers profound leadership lessons. Standing only a few inches tall, its spines are more playful than menacing, yet they hold a metaphor for resilience and resourcefulness within them. Like the cactus, leaders can thrive in adversity, adapting and innovating to overcome challenges while tapping into their inner reserves to create opportunities.

Resourcefulness in leadership goes beyond simply surviving difficult situations. It involves setting boundaries, knowing when to conserve energy, and leveraging adversity to your advantage. With its prickly exterior, the cactus is a powerful symbol of resourcefulness. Its spines are both a defense mechanism and a means to define its space, protect its resources, and ensure survival. Similarly, leaders must learn to establish healthy boundaries, prioritize their well-being, and transform challenges into catalysts for growth.

This chapter explores the connection between the cactus's resilience and a leader's resourcefulness. It examines how we can harness our inner strength, set effective boundaries, and turn obstacles into opportunities, enabling us to thrive in the unpredictable terrain of leadership.

Like the Arctic fox, the cactus survives and thrives in harsh climates. For example, the Saguaro Cactus, native to the Sonoran Desert, is the largest in the United States, reaching heights of 10 to 40 feet. Its root system can extend as far as 100 feet, enabling it to survive with as little as 3 inches of rain annually. These remarkable plants can live for up to 200 years, a testament to their resilience and ability to thrive in even the most challenging environments. Similarly, great leaders can endure and succeed through resourcefulness, adaptability, and strategic resilience.

This plant, a master of adaptation and survival, offers valuable lessons for leaders. By examining the cactus's remarkable strategies and applying its lessons to our leadership styles, we can unlock the secrets to thriving in adversity, optimizing resources, and fostering a culture of resilience. In its quiet strength, the cactus invites us to explore the profound connection between nature's wisdom and the art of leadership.

The cactus is a master of resource management, particularly in the harsh desert environment where water is scarce. It has evolved unique adaptations to conserve every precious drop. Its thick, fleshy stem is a reservoir, storing water for extended periods. Its spines, often perceived as defense mechanisms, minimize surface area and create shade, helping to reduce water loss.

Leaders can learn the importance of identifying and valuing their resources—time, talent, or financial capital from the cactus. Just as the cactus maximizes every drop of water to survive, influential leaders understand the need to optimize resources, minimize waste, and ensure long-term sustainability. The cactus teaches us that true strength lies not in abundance but in the ability to make the most of what we have, ensuring we thrive despite adversity.

Beyond resource management, the cactus's ability to thrive in adversity showcases its resourcefulness. It survives and flourishes under scorching heat, in arid conditions, and in nutrient-poor soil. Its roots spread wide and shallow, maximizing its ability to capture moisture, while its photosynthesis process is highly efficient even in limited sunlight. Leaders can emulate this adaptability by cultivating a mindset that views challenges as opportunities for growth. Rather than succumbing to adversity, resourceful leaders find innovative ways to overcome obstacles, transforming setbacks into stepping stones. This perspective allows them to leverage their circumstances and create new paths forward.

The cactus's growth strategy also provides a valuable lesson: it avoids rapid, unsustainable expansion, focusing instead on slow, steady growth. It invests its energy wisely, prioritizing survival over unnecessary extravagance. This measured approach ensures its longevity in an unpredictable environment. Leaders can adopt this principle by setting realistic goals, making informed decisions, and avoiding impulsive actions. Sustainable growth requires building a solid foundation, nurturing relationships, and fostering a culture of continuous improvement. Like the cactus, leaders who pace their growth can weather challenges and remain resilient.

One of the greatest challenges leaders face is establishing and maintaining healthy boundaries. Often, especially for those who prioritize servant leadership, there is a tendency to feel the need to have all the answers and act immediately. The spines of the cactus remind us of the importance of setting boundaries. While they may appear intimidating, they are vital for the cactus's survival. They deter predators, shield the plant from excessive sunlight, and reduce water loss. Similarly, leaders must learn to protect their time, energy, and resources by setting clear boundaries, allowing for personal well-being, and fostering a more sustainable leadership approach. Like the cactus's spines, these boundaries help maintain the balance necessary for long-term success and survival.

Similarly, leaders must establish and maintain healthy boundaries in their personal and professional lives. While it can be challenging, setting boundaries involves learning to say no to unreasonable demands, effectively delegating tasks, and protecting time and energy for what truly matters. Clear boundaries foster respect, prevent burnout, and ensure leaders have the resources and mental space to lead effectively. Just like the cactus's spines, which define its space and protect it from external forces, leaders must define their limits and safeguard their well-being to ensure sustained success.

The cactus's adaptability is central to its resourcefulness. Over time, it has evolved to thrive in ever-changing environments, adjusting its strategies to manage temperature, rainfall, and sunlight fluctuations. This plant exemplifies remarkable innovation, continuously finding new ways to capture and conserve resources. Leaders who embrace adaptability and innovation are better equipped to navigate the complexities of today's modern world. They remain open to new ideas, willing to experiment, and agile in adjusting their approach to changing circumstances. By fostering a culture of innovation, leaders prepare their teams to approach challenges with creativity and flexibility, turning uncertainty into opportunity.

As a stoic survivor of harsh environments, the cactus offers profound lessons in resilience and resourcefulness, particularly its ability to transform adversity into opportunity. Despite the scorching heat, arid conditions, and limited resources, the cactus survives, showcasing its extraordinary capacity to adapt and innovate. Leaders can draw valuable lessons from this remarkable trait, learning how to approach adversity with a mindset of opportunity. Leaders who embody resilience and resourcefulness can inspire their teams to persevere, ensuring setbacks are viewed as stepping stones to greater success.

The core of the cactus's resilience lies in its remarkable ability to leverage adversity as a catalyst for growth. In the harsh desert environment, where extreme temperatures and scarce water supplies create significant challenges, the cactus has evolved ingenious adaptations that allow it to survive and thrive.

For instance, the cactus's spines serve as a defense mechanism and a survival strategy. While they may appear purely protective, the spines perform a critical function in conserving water. They create shade, which helps reduce water loss through transpiration and trap moisture from the air, guiding it toward the plant's roots. In this way, the cactus turns an otherwise hostile element—the sun's intense heat—into a valuable resource supporting survival.

Similarly, the cactus's shallow, widespread root system cleverly adapts to its environment. While this may seem like a disadvantage regarding stability, it allows the cactus to absorb any available moisture from infrequent rainfall quickly. By spreading its roots across a broad area, the cactus maximizes its chances of capturing water, even in the driest conditions. This adaptation ensures that the cactus remains resilient and resourceful, ready to take advantage of whatever opportunities arise, no matter how fleeting or unpredictable.

These adaptations exemplify the cactus's ability to turn adversity into an advantage. The cactus does not merely endure harsh conditions; it leverages them to thrive. This resilience highlights the cactus's extraordinary adaptability and ability to solve seemingly impossible challenges creatively. In an environment where most life forms would struggle, the cactus flourishes using elements others might view as obstacles.

Leaders can draw profound lessons from the cactus's approach to adversity. Resourceful leaders don't react impulsively when faced with setbacks, challenges, or unexpected obstacles; they respond strategically. They take the time to assess the situation, identify opportunities, and leverage their available resources to turn adversity into an advantage. Just as the cactus turns harsh sunlight into life-sustaining moisture, leaders can find ways to transform challenges into growth opportunities.

The cactus's example also underscores the importance of maintaining a long-term perspective. While short-term setbacks may seem daunting or discouraging, they often set the stage for long-term growth. The cactus's slow, steady growth and its ability to endure prolonged droughts speak to the power of resilience and sustainability. Similarly, leaders who focus on building resilience and sustainability rather than rushing for quick wins are better positioned to weather temporary storms and emerge stronger and more capable in the long run. The cactus reminds us that lasting success often requires patience and the ability to adapt over time.

During a time of significant supply chain disruptions, I had the opportunity to work with a leadership team that, like the cactus, turned adversity into an advantage. In a strategy session, the team pivoted quickly and transformed the supply chain disruption into an opportunity to diversify suppliers. They found ways to grow despite the challenges by being resourceful and agile. This shift in perspective demonstrated the power of viewing adversity through the lens of opportunity. The key is approaching challenges with curiosity, creativity, and resilience. Leaders who adopt this mindset can unlock their full potential and guide their organizations to new heights.

The cactus embodies the adage, "What doesn't kill you makes you stronger." Its ability to survive and thrive in the harshest conditions—adapting to its environment, utilizing scarce resources, and managing adversity—offers a powerful lesson for leaders across all fields. Just as the cactus turns obstacles into opportunities for growth, leaders can apply similar principles to their leadership approach. By embracing the cactus's wisdom, we can transform adversity into an advantage and achieve sustainable success.

Though seemingly simple, the cactus becomes an unexpected mentor in leadership. Its ability to navigate adversity, manage resources effectively, set boundaries, and adapt to changing conditions provides invaluable lessons for leaders in any industry. By incorporating these strategies into our leadership styles, we cultivate resilience, resourcefulness, and adaptability—key traits for thriving in today's complex world. As we confront the challenges and opportunities ahead, we should remember the cactus: a quiet yet powerful testament to the virtues of perseverance, innovation, and the relentless pursuit of growth. In its silent strength, we find inspiration to lead with purpose, clarity, and a deep respect for the resources at our disposal.

Leadership Reflections:

1. How can I evolve and adapt my leadership style?

- Seek feedback regularly from my team to understand areas of improvement and adapt my approach accordingly.
- Stay open to new leadership techniques, such as incorporating emotional intelligence or coaching practices into my daily interactions.
- Monitor industry trends and adjust my leadership style to meet the changing demands of my organization and the market.

2. What are some additional ways I can be more efficient?

- Prioritize tasks based on impact and delegate effectively to ensure focus on high-value activities.
- Implement technology tools to streamline communication, project management, and workflow processes.
- Set clear and measurable goals to track progress, identify bottlenecks, and refine processes for greater efficiency.

3. What is my strategy for navigating boundaries?

- Establish clear expectations and limits with my team, ensuring everyone understands their roles and responsibilities.
- Learn to refuse requests that conflict with my core objectives or compromise my well-being.
- Practice assertiveness in maintaining work-life balance, ensuring personal time is respected, and work demands are manageable.

Micro Actions:

- I will consciously reframe difficult situations as opportunities for growth and encourage my team to do the same.
- I will conduct a resource audit to identify areas for optimization or reallocation to support long-term goals.
- I will establish a boundary protection strategy that fosters respect and prevents burnout.

INTUITION

"Look deep into nature, and then you will understand everything better."

—Albert Einstein

Nature Provides Opportunity to Follow Your Intuition

CHAPTER 7

COLLABORATIVE LEADERSHIP

When I moved to the Finger Lakes region of New York, I never expected to become a birdwatcher. However, birdwatching has become a form of meditation for me, offering a glimpse into the intricate workings of nature. Each chirp and rustle grounds me in the present moment, reminding me of the beauty surrounding us.

In the autumn, during migration, I often watch flocks of cedar waxwings navigate the branches of the spruce trees in our forest. Their effortless grace and extraordinary teamwork are mesmerizing. Their movements are seamless, and their communication almost seems telepathic. Each bird understands its role, contributing to the collective effort of finding food and ensuring the flock's survival. I marvel at how they dart and weave, instinctively knowing when to lead and when to follow, creating a dynamic yet harmonious dance that allows them to thrive.

This captivating display sparks my curiosity every autumn: Could these birds offer leadership lessons? Could their instinctive collaboration teach us to become better collaborators ourselves? Their very existence is built on trust and instinct. Each bird relies on its companions, just as we must depend on one another professionally. The flock's success is a powerful metaphor for any team or organization. When each member is empowered to contribute their unique strengths, the whole becomes greater than the sum of its parts.

Exploring bird behavior unveils a treasure trove of wisdom—a blueprint for collaborative leadership written in the sky. Watching the waxwings, I am struck by their ability to communicate effortlessly. They engage in a complex system of vocalizations and subtle body movements, ensuring everyone is aligned. Creating an environment where team members feel safe to express ideas and concerns can lead to innovative solutions and a more cohesive unit. Just as the birds maintain their connection through constant interaction, we, too, must foster a culture of dialogue and understanding to keep our teams united.

Birds adapt to their environment and one another in a way that underscores the importance of flexibility in leadership. They instinctively adjust their strategies based on factors like food availability or the presence of potential threats, displaying an agility we can all learn from. Pivoting to changing circumstances with agility is crucial. A leader who embraces adaptability fosters resilience within their team, equipping them to navigate uncertainty confidently. The cedar waxwings remind me that collaboration is not static but dynamic, requiring continuous evolution and adjustment together.

Bird flocks also remind us that leadership isn't just about providing direction; it's about creating a shared vision. While each bird contributes individually, they work toward a common goal, demonstrating the power of unity. This collective purpose enhances productivity and builds a sense of belonging. In organizations, when team members understand and buy into a shared mission, they are more likely to invest their time and energy, making meaningful contributions toward achieving it.

Birds remind me that nature is not just a backdrop to our lives but a rich source of profound insights. The lessons of the cedar waxwings stay with me long after I observe their migration. By embracing teamwork, communication, adaptability, and shared purpose, we can cultivate a thriving collaborative environment that empowers everyone to soar.

The seamless coordination of a flock arises from a blend of instinct and learned behavior. Birds instinctively follow the movements of their neighbors, creating a ripple effect throughout the group. They communicate through subtle cues, like wing movements or vocalizations, to share information about threats or food sources. A remarkable example is the murmur of starlings—thousands of birds swirling and diving in unison, creating a spectacle that seems to defy explanation. Yet, scientists have found that each bird reacts to the movements of its closest neighbors, creating a complex pattern from simple reactions. This shows how collaboration can produce extraordinary results even when driven by instinct.

The beauty of this coordinated movement lies not only in its visual appeal but also in its efficiency and effectiveness. Each bird, while maintaining its individuality, contributes to the greater good of the flock. There's no jostling for position or conflict over resources. Instead, there's a shared understanding that individual success is intrinsically tied to the group's success.

In the human world, this mirrors the importance of creating a shared vision and clear goals within a team. As birds move toward a common direction, team members must align with a shared purpose. Achieving alignment requires clear communication, ensuring everyone understands their role and how it contributes to the bigger picture. This sense of shared direction fosters cooperation, minimizes friction, and helps propel the team toward its collective goals.

Seamless coordination requires a culture of open communication and feedback. Just as birds use subtle cues to communicate, team members must feel comfortable sharing information and providing feedback to one another. This open exchange fosters an environment where potential issues are addressed early, preventing them from escalating into larger problems.

Beyond coordination, birds teach another vital lesson: the art of adaptation. Birds are highly attuned to their surroundings, constantly scanning for danger and opportunity. They use their keen senses—sight, hearing, and even smell—to gather information and make informed decisions based on instinct and intuition. For example, geese have been observed altering their migration routes in response to shifting weather patterns, ensuring they reach their destination safely.

This heightened awareness allows birds to respond quickly to changing conditions. When a predator approaches, the flock scatters in a coordinated manner, improving individual survival chances. Conversely, they converge remarkably when discovering a food source, working together toward a shared goal.

Sensing and adapting are equally critical for business success. Leaders must remain attuned to the shifting landscape—market conditions, customer needs, and technological advancements. Leaders can make informed, agile decisions by gathering information from diverse sources, analyzing it critically, and blending data with intuition.

Just as birds alter their flight paths in response to changing weather, leaders must stay flexible and adaptable in their strategies. What worked yesterday may no longer be effective today. The ability to pivot and adjust course when necessary distinguishes successful leaders from those who fail to keep up with change.

Finally, the most profound lesson from the birds may be the importance of empowering and trusting others. Each bird plays a vital role in the flock, regardless of size or strength. While the leader sets the direction and makes critical decisions, they rely on the collective wisdom and abilities of the entire flock to achieve their goals. This trust and empowerment allow the birds to share information and responsibilities seamlessly.

For example, when one bird finds a food source, it alerts the rest of the flock. When a predator approaches, the birds work together to defend themselves. This collaborative approach ensures that the flock, as a whole, is stronger and more resilient than any individual bird could be alone.

In leadership, this underscores the importance of empowering team members and trusting their abilities. Micromanaging and hoarding control stifle creativity and innovation. Instead, leaders should create an environment where team members feel empowered to take initiative, make decisions, and contribute their unique talents to the greater mission.

Empowerment also requires cultivating a culture of trust and respect. Team members must feel comfortable sharing their ideas and opinions without fear of judgment or ridicule. They must know their contributions are valued and their leader has their back.

The birds remind me that we are interconnected beings who thrive within a community. They teach me that by working together, sharing information, and trusting one another's abilities, we can achieve far more than we could alone.

Just as each bird contributes to the flock's success, we contribute to the success of our teams, organizations, and communities. By embracing the lessons of the flock—coordination, adaptability, empowerment, and trust—we can make collaboration more than just a buzzword; it becomes a way of life.

Leadership Reflections:

1. **What can I do to encourage greater collaboration with my team?**
   - Foster open communication: Encourage regular check-ins and create a space where team members feel comfortable sharing ideas.
   - Set clear team goals: Ensure everyone understands the common objective and how their contributions help achieve it.
   - Recognize collaborative efforts: Celebrate team successes and acknowledge when collaboration leads to impactful results.

2. **What is my practice in delegating?**
   - Trust team members with responsibility: Assign tasks based on individual strengths and trust them to handle the work independently.
   - Provide clear expectations: Set clear goals and timelines to ensure everyone knows what is expected and when it's due.
   - Offer support when needed: Be available for guidance but avoid micromanaging, allowing team members the autonomy to succeed.

3. **What is the value of adapting my leadership style to be more collaborative?**

   - Builds stronger relationships: Collaboration fosters trust and respect, strengthening team cohesion and performance.

   - Encourages innovation: A collaborative leadership style can lead to more creative and effective solutions by leveraging diverse perspectives.

   - Increases team engagement: When members feel included and heard, they are more motivated to contribute and perform at their best.

Micro Actions:

- I will delegate a task that I usually handle myself.
- I will actively seek feedback from my team.
- I will recognize and celebrate individual and team accomplishments.

CHAPTER 8

VIGILANCE AND SUSTAINABILITY

When I was seven, my father came home with a beehive and a large wooden structure, a trade he made for some house painting. I remember helping him pull it out of the back of a truck, the hive draped with one of his old painting drop cloths. What struck me most was the vibration of the wooden box, a subtle hum that seemed to pulse with life. As the season unfolded, my father honed his skills as a beekeeper, learning the nuances of tending to the hive. I enjoyed those moments, often at his side, watching him grow into a seasoned caretaker of bees. Though a man of few words, my father deeply respected these creatures and their intricate society. Through him, I learned the delicate art of beekeeping and absorbed invaluable lessons about vigilance, sustainability, and leadership that would shape my views on life.

The sheer organization within the hive was captivating. Each bee knew its role and executed it precisely—whether foraging for food, defending the hive, or nurturing the larvae. This intricate system created a living tapestry, vibrant and humbling in its perfection. My father's decision to become a beekeeper allowed me to witness one of nature's most beautiful dances—a dance of purpose, coordination, and collaboration.

The harmony within the hive taught me powerful lessons about teamwork and the significance of each individual's contribution to a shared goal. He often explained that the hive's survival depended on the collective efforts of every bee, with each playing a vital role in the hive's intricate life. His words stayed with me: no task was too small; every bee mattered. In the same way, effective leaders recognize the importance of every team member, understanding that each person's contribution is essential to the success of the collective effort.

He taught me that leadership, like beekeeping, requires a keen eye for detail, a deep understanding of interconnectedness, and the courage to make tough decisions. Just as the queen bee leads the colony with trust and respect, a good leader fosters an environment where team members feel empowered and valued, creating a culture where open communication can flourish. Ideas flow freely in an empowered environment, much like bees gathering nectar. Effective leadership also means being attuned to the subtle shifts within a group—recognizing when motivation wanes, or conflicts emerge and knowing how to address these challenges with sensitivity and insight. Just as a beekeeper regularly inspects the hive to ensure its health, a leader must remain vigilant, responsive to the team's evolving needs, and proactive in maintaining the well-being of the collective.

The bees' unwavering focus on their tasks also highlighted the importance of resilience. When faced with adversity—environmental changes or predator threats—they adapt and work together to overcome challenges. This adaptability is a crucial lesson for any leader; it reinforces the idea that flexibility and a problem-solving mindset are essential for navigating the complexities of professional life. Just as bees quickly devise strategies to protect their hive, leaders must foster similar agility within their teams, encouraging creative solutions and collaborative efforts to meet challenges head-on.

Observing the bees also taught me the beauty of shared success. When the hive thrives, every bee benefits and the bounty is shared among all community members. Applying the principles of shared success to the workplace helps create a culture that celebrates collective achievements, boosts morale, and strengthens relationships among team members. Witnessing my father's respect for the bees taught me that leadership is about service—supporting others and prioritizing the collective good over individual accolades. Ultimately, these lessons from the hive have shaped my understanding of effective leadership and the qualities necessary to cultivate a thriving community, whether in nature or our professional endeavors.

One of the most remarkable aspects of bee behavior is their unwavering vigilance. Bees remain constantly alert, scanning for threats like predators, pests, or environmental changes. Their vigilance is not just reactive but proactive and strategic. I marveled at how guard bees would stand sentinel at the entrance, ever watchful, ensuring the hive remained safe from intruders. Their communication system, which relies on pheromones and intricate dances, allows them to share crucial information about threats and resources in real time. This constant awareness and readiness ensures the hive can respond quickly and effectively to any challenge.

For example, guard bees stationed at the hive's entrance meticulously inspect every incoming bee, ensuring only authorized members are allowed inside. They also patrol the perimeter of the hive, scanning the surroundings for any signs of danger. This vigilance, coupled with their sophisticated communication methods, ensures that the hive remains protected and the colony continues to thrive. It's a powerful reminder that vigilance—monitoring our environment and staying connected with our teams—is a fundamental element of effective leadership.

However, vigilance isn't their only strength. The beehive is also a model of sustainability, a testament to the bees' ability to manage resources efficiently and ensure the long-term health of their community. I learned that bees carefully collect nectar and pollen from various flowers, ensuring they don't deplete any single source. They store surplus honey for lean times, guaranteeing the hive has enough food to survive the winter months. Additionally, they regulate the temperature and humidity of the hive, creating a stable environment that promotes the health and productivity of the colony. This sustainable approach benefits the bees directly but also contributes to pollinating crops and supporting broader biodiversity, highlighting their role in ecosystems' interconnectedness.

The intricate honeycomb structure within the hive is a testament to the bee's engineering prowess. Each hexagonal cell is perfectly designed to maximize storage capacity while minimizing the wax required. As I observed the bees working, I couldn't help but admire their architectural skill; it blended artistry and functionality almost flawlessly. The bees' ability to regulate the temperature within the hive is equally impressive. They use their wings to fan air and circulate it throughout the hive, maintaining a consistent temperature optimal for brood rearing and honey production.

This ability to adapt and create a stable environment speaks volumes about their resilience, intelligence, and commitment to long-term sustainability—principles from which any leader can draw inspiration when considering building and nurturing a thriving, adaptable team.

The ability to make swift decisions is another hallmark of the beehive. Bees are known for their decisiveness, especially when protecting the hive. I witnessed this firsthand during one hot afternoon when I saw a wasp attempting to invade the hive. Without hesitation, the bees immediately banded together, swarming the intruder and driving it away. It was a clear demonstration of their collective resolve and quick action. As leaders, we may not be able to eliminate all threats, but we can take a page from the bees' book by remaining vigilant in setting boundaries for ourselves and our teams. We must also be prepared to take decisive action when the situation demands it, whether addressing a challenge or seizing an opportunity.

For example, when the hive needs to choose a new nesting site, scout bees explore potential locations and return to the hive to communicate their findings through a series of dances. The intensity and duration of the dance convey the quality of the site, and the bees ultimately decide on the best option through a process of consensus. This collaborative decision-making process, combined with the bees' ability to act quickly once a decision is made, highlights the importance of clear communication, alignment, and trust within a team. By fostering an environment where everyone feels empowered to share their insights and contribute to the decision-making process, leaders can strengthen their team's ability to act decisively and confidently move forward.

Reflecting on my father's lessons about beekeeping and my leadership experiences, I draw inspiration from the bees' ability to work harmoniously toward a common goal. The beehive, a microcosm of collaboration, resilience, and resourcefulness, offers profound wisdom for effective leadership. We can build prosperous, resilient, and purpose-driven organizations by embracing the bee's vigilance, sustainability, and decisiveness.

The beehive teaches us that leadership is not about individual power or authority; it's about fostering a collective spirit, empowering others, and working together towards a common goal. This collaborative spirit encourages innovation and creativity as diverse perspectives come together to solve challenges. Leaders should cultivate an environment where every team member feels empowered to contribute unique insights, like the bees' roles within the hive.

It's about creating a culture of vigilance, where everyone is attuned to potential threats and opportunities. Just as bees communicate with one another through their intricate dances, leaders must ensure open lines of communication, making sure that every team member feels heard and valued. Effective leadership fosters a sense of shared responsibility, where everyone's input contributes to the team's overall success.

Sustainability is another critical lesson. Just as bees manage their resources wisely to ensure the hive's longevity, leaders must be mindful of the long-term impact of their decisions. It's essential to act to support future generations' well-being and maintain a healthy, thriving organization.

Lastly, it's about making decisive decisions, even when uncertain or adversity. Just as bees instinctively protect their hive, leaders must cultivate the confidence to make tough calls when necessary, trusting their team's collective wisdom and strength. This decisiveness doesn't negate the need for thoughtful deliberation but enhances a leader's ability to act swiftly and effectively during moments of crisis. These lessons from the hive offer profound insights into leadership—how we lead, connect, and inspire others in our professional and personal lives.

In essence, the principles embodied by the bees serve as a roadmap for effective leadership. When we adopt a mindset of vigilance, we become more attuned to our environment, creating a culture that fosters proactive action rather than reacting to challenges after they arise. By prioritizing sustainability, we build systems that thrive today while ensuring future generations can continue to flourish. Making decisive choices empowers us and our teams, enabling us to navigate the complexities of leadership with clarity and purpose.

Reflecting on my father's teachings and the bees' lessons, I feel deeply grateful for nature's wisdom. These lessons extend beyond beekeeping; they resonate with anyone seeking to lead effectively in an ever-changing world. They remind us that leadership is not a solitary journey but a collective effort that requires commitment, respect, and a willingness to learn from those around us. Embracing these principles can transform our approach to leadership, allowing us to cultivate environments that inspire creativity, foster resilience, and empower others to reach their fullest potential.

Leadership Reflections:

1. **What challenges and opportunities am I noticing in my current environment?**
   - **Challenges:**
     - The increasing complexity of cross-functional collaboration requires more alignment between departments.
     - Rising competition and market shifts demand quicker adaptability and innovation.
     - Difficulty maintaining team motivation and focus amid changing priorities.
   - **Opportunities:**
     - Implementing more flexible work models to adapt to the team's evolving needs.

○ Harnessing AI tools to streamline workflows and improve efficiency.

○ Building stronger relationships with stakeholders by emphasizing transparent communication.

2. What is my style when making tough decisions?

- **Consultative:** I seek input from key stakeholders before considering all perspectives.

- **Data-driven:** I rely on available data and analytics to make informed, objective decisions, minimizing personal bias.

- **Decisive:** Once the decision is made, I act quickly and confidently to avoid delays and maintain momentum.

3. What can I do to foster decisiveness in my team?

- **Encourage autonomy:** Empower team members to make decisions within their areas of expertise, building their confidence in their judgment.

- **Set clear expectations:** Clarify roles, objectives, and timelines so the team has the framework to make quick, informed decisions.

- **Support risk-taking:** Create a safe environment where calculated risks are encouraged and mistakes are viewed as learning opportunities.

Micro Actions:

- I will conduct regular environmental scans and routinely monitor industry trends, competitor activity, and emerging challenges to foster vigilance and ensure I am proactive, not reactive, to potential threats or opportunities.

- I will promote sustainable practices within my team by encouraging resource conservation, maintaining a balanced workload for team well-being, and making decisions with long-term impact in mind.
- I will encourage quick, informed decision-making. I will cultivate an environment where my team feels empowered to make decisions and support them in acting confidently.

CHAPTER 9

THE CURIOUS EXPLORER

I was a health educator specializing in substance abuse education early in my career. I was fortunate to be invited to the University of North Carolina at Wilmington for several consecutive summers to teach a week-long course to other health professionals. The university housed us in apartment-style dormitories. Each summer, I had the same two roommates: a psychiatrist from Duke University and a Doctor of Applied Coastal and Ocean Sciences. During our time together, I learned much about mindfulness meditation from the psychiatrist, but that is a topic for another book!

The professor's research focused on animal behavior and marine ecology, particularly octopuses and their relatives. Of course, from watching *The Undersea World of Jacques Cousteau* as a young man, I knew a little about octopuses. However, what I learned over a few summers changed my perspective on these intriguing creatures and later served as a lens for examining leadership.

The octopus embodies curiosity in its most vivid form. With eight flexible arms and keen intelligence, these creatures exhibit remarkable curiosity and exploration. They engage with their surroundings in ways that reveal sensory clarity, problem-solving skills, and curiosity—hallmarks of effective leadership.

The octopus has unique sensory organs and perceives its environment with exceptional clarity. Each of its arms is lined with thousands of sensitive suckers, capable of both tasting and feeling simultaneously. This heightened sensory perception enables the octopus to explore its world in great detail, picking up on subtleties often unnoticed by other creatures. When an octopus encounters a new object, it goes beyond mere observation; it interacts, investigates, and learns, demonstrating an engagement with the world that is both systematic and imaginative. It can change color and texture, adapting its appearance to blend into its surroundings, showcasing a mastery of camouflage that highlights its ability to assess and respond to its environment in real time.

This capacity for sensory engagement reminds me of the importance of being fully present as a leader. Losing sight of the details in our fast-paced, often overwhelming world is easy. However, as the octopus uses its senses to navigate complex underwater landscapes, influential leaders must hone their ability to observe and interpret the dynamics within their teams and organizations. Awareness involves noticing verbal and non-verbal signals—such as body language and emotional undertones—that can influence group dynamics. Like a wise octopus, a keen leader can sense when team members are disengaged or tension is simmering beneath the surface. By developing this awareness, leaders can foster a more open and collaborative environment, leading to more effective decision-making and stronger team cohesion.

One of the most impressive aspects of octopus behavior is its remarkable problem-solving abilities. In various studies, these intelligent creatures have escaped from enclosures, opened jars, and even used tools, demonstrating a level of cognitive sophistication that continues to astonish scientists. Their problem-solving skills are driven by curiosity, prompting them to experiment with different approaches until they find a solution. For instance, when faced with a challenging situation, an octopus may try several strategies: it might change its shape to squeeze through a narrow opening, use its tentacles to manipulate an object, or even employ distraction techniques to evade a predator. The octopus's adaptability and curiosity allow it to thrive in diverse and often unpredictable marine ecosystems.

For leaders, fostering a culture of problem-solving is crucial. Encouraging team members to think creatively and explore new ideas can lead to innovative solutions. When leaders create an environment where experimentation is accepted and celebrated, they inspire their teams to take calculated risks and push boundaries. Just as the octopus demonstrates resilience and adaptability when faced with challenges, leaders should cultivate a culture that embraces exploration and supports continuous learning, providing the resources and opportunities necessary for team members to develop their skills through training, collaboration, or simply creating space for dialogue and brainstorming.

Curiosity is the heartbeat of the octopus's existence. It explores its environment with an eagerness that is essential for survival. Each new experience enriches its understanding of the world, enabling it to navigate its habitat skillfully and confidently. This exploration is not just about survival; it's a quest for knowledge that reflects an intricate relationship with its surroundings. The octopus's ability to adapt to various challenges is a testament to its curiosity, allowing it to utilize resources innovatively. Whether investigating a new object or navigating unfamiliar territory, the octopus's curiosity drives it to learn and grow. This innate drive benefits the individual octopus and contributes to the overall health of the marine ecosystem. A curious octopus is an engaged participant in its environment, helping to maintain the balance of life within the ocean. Exploring different nooks and crannies of its habitat can uncover hidden food sources and help keep the ecosystem thriving.

In the realm of leadership, curiosity is equally vital. Leaders who embrace curiosity are more likely to challenge the status quo and seek new growth opportunities. This mindset is not simply about asking questions; it involves a deep commitment to understanding others' perspectives and insights. Leaders can gain a more comprehensive view of challenges and possibilities by actively listening and seeking diverse viewpoints. This approach encourages open dialogue, creative thinking, and collaboration, enabling teams to adapt to changing circumstances and innovate. When leaders model curiosity, they empower their teams to ask questions, explore new ideas, and engage in meaningful discussions.

An environment that invites questioning creates a psychological safety essential for innovation. Team members feel valued and are more willing to share their thoughts without fear of judgment, leading to a richer pool of ideas and solutions. In such a culture, curiosity becomes contagious; as leaders exhibit their inquisitiveness, team members often adopt a similar mindset. This collective curiosity enhances problem-solving capabilities and fosters a sense of ownership and investment among team members. When individuals feel their contributions matter, they are more likely to be engaged and committed to the team's success.

A curious leader is an adaptable leader. Leaders who encourage curiosity can better navigate uncertainties and complexities and are open to learning from failures and successes. Leaders willing to experiment, iterate, and be vulnerable embody a deeper understanding of their ecosystem. Just as the octopus uses its intelligence and adaptability to thrive in various marine environments, leaders can harness the power of curiosity to ensure their organizations remain relevant and resilient.

Curiosity catalyzes growth, both for the individual and the team. By nurturing this trait within ourselves and our teams, we create an atmosphere where exploration, creativity, and collaboration flourish. The lessons drawn from the octopus remind us that, like them, we must embrace our curiosity to navigate the complexities of our environments, enrich our understanding, and ultimately lead with insight and empathy. Curiosity can help leaders navigate uncertainty and complexity. In a constantly evolving world, leaders must be willing to explore unfamiliar territory, and by remaining curious and open to learning, they can adapt their strategies and approaches to meet their challenges. This flexibility is essential. In many instances, traditional solutions may no longer apply. When faced with a novel situation, an octopus does not retreat; it engages and explores, embodying the spirit of discovery that leaders should aspire to emulate.

Reflecting on my own experiences, I see how curiosity has played a pivotal role in my journey. In many ways, my career path has been fueled by curiosity. My first career pursuit was as an investment banker, a field I became curious about after seeing my father make a little extra money in the stock market. When I examine my career moves over time—shifting from investment banking to health education, healthcare administration, finance, human resources, and now my current pursuits—I see that curiosity spurred each of these transitions. The moments when I allowed myself to explore new ideas, challenge my assumptions, and seek out diverse perspectives have led to some of the most significant breakthroughs in my personal and professional development. Each time I embraced the unknown, I discovered new opportunities for growth and connection.

In its natural habitat, the octopus reminds me of the beauty and excitement of exploration. The ocean is vast and mysterious, filled with hidden treasures and unknown challenges. The octopus approaches this environment with wonder and adventure, confidently diving into the depths. It invites us to do the same in our lives, approaching each day with curiosity and a willingness to explore. Whether we are navigating the complexities of our relationships or the intricacies of our professional endeavors, embracing curiosity can open doors to new possibilities and insight.

Ultimately, the octopus is a powerful symbol of the qualities that make influential leaders. Its sensory clarity, problem-solving skills, and insatiable curiosity remind us of the importance of engaging with our environment and embracing exploration. By cultivating these qualities within ourselves and fostering them in our teams, we can create a culture that thrives on creativity, collaboration, and continuous growth.

The ocean depths may be daunting, but like the octopus, we have the potential to navigate the unknown with confidence, curiosity, and resilience. Through this journey of discovery, we can deepen our understanding of ourselves, our teams, and the world around us, ultimately leading us toward a more vibrant and fulfilling existence. The lessons of the octopus extend beyond the water; they resonate deeply in our lives, urging us to explore, learn, and lead with a sense of wonder.

Leadership Reflections:

1. **How can I enhance my sensory awareness as a leader?**
   - Actively listen to verbal and non-verbal cues from team members.
   - Observe group dynamics and seek to understand underlying emotions or tensions.
   - Stay present in interactions to detect subtle mood, energy, or motivation changes within the team.

2. **What can I do to encourage an environment of creative solutions?**
   - Foster a culture where experimentation and risk-taking are encouraged, not punished.
   - Provide the team with the resources, time, and freedom to brainstorm and explore new ideas.
   - Recognize and celebrate innovative thinking, reinforcing that creative solutions are valued.

3. **How can I encourage exploration and learning among my team members?**
   - Create opportunities for team members to explore new areas of knowledge, such as through training, cross-functional collaboration, or mentorship.
   - To support continuous learning, provide access to resources that promote growth, such as courses, books, or conferences.
   - Cultivate a mindset of curiosity by modeling it in your actions and asking thoughtful questions that provoke deeper thinking.

Micro Actions:

- I will observe my team's interactions and note any non-verbal signals or dynamics I may have overlooked.
- I will organize regular brainstorming sessions where team members can propose unconventional solutions to existing challenges.
- I will create a "question of the week" initiative where team members can pose their most curious inquiries about their work or the organization. I will address these questions openly to foster a culture of curiosity.

MOVING FORWARD

"I see no more than you, but I have trained myself to notice what I see."

—Sherlock Holmes

I Look to the Future

CHAPTER 10

MOVING FORWARD

Congratulations! You've taken a significant step in honing your leadership skills for the future.

During my childhood adventures with my grandparents, we often traveled to camp on their property in the North Carolina mountains, on the border with Tennessee. When I climbed to the top of the hill from our camper, I could see across the border and mountains into Tennessee. In those quiet moments, I often reflected on my childhood and my hopes for my future. Life has taken a lot of turns, some very sharp, but I always return to nature for inspiration and solace.

Throughout my career, I've had the honor and privilege of serving in two distinct C-Suite roles: Chief Financial Officer and Chief Human Resources Officer. When I reflect, it is clear to me that the leadership lessons of adaptability, resilience, and intuition are the capabilities that will define the future of leadership. In an era of misinformation, cultivating our natural abilities to adapt, be resilient, and honor our intuition can make all the difference.

My grandparents taught me to observe the subtleties of the natural world. In doing so, they gave me a gift that continues to serve me and those around me. I never imagined strolling around a garden in the summer evening and hearing my grandparents tell me about the flowers and the trees would profoundly impact my life. I hope you are encouraged and inspired to seek inspiration in the wild. However, you define it. For me, the wild is the forest surrounding my home. Other times, when traveling, the wild might be a local park, green space, or simply a tree on the sidewalk.

Throughout this book, I have shared the aspects of nature that inspire me. I encourage you to seek your sources of inspiration, whether it's the beauty of a sunrise or sunset, the feel of a gentle breeze on a warm summer day, or the unconditional love of a pet. I hope that by connecting with nature, you'll uncover new perspectives and insights that enrich your journey like:

- Adaptability to and navigating change.
- Building resilience to overcome challenges.
- You are honoring and trusting your intuition to make decisions in uncertainty.

You don't need leadership development, coaching, a seminar, a podcast, a book (even this one!), a course, or a social media platform to develop these capabilities; they are already part of who you are. We can rediscover These innate abilities by paying attention to the world.

Leadership is often chaotic and rife with uncertainty. In all its raw and unpredictable beauty, nature thrives through interconnectedness, balance, and an ability to adjust in real time. When we embrace these qualities, we foster personal growth and create environments where our teams can flourish.

I invite you to reconnect with the natural world and yourself in many ways. As leaders, when we learn to listen to the whispers of the wind, trust the flow of the seasons, and observe the resilience of life in all its forms, we begin to embody the future-focused competencies we seek. We become more intuitive, adaptable, and resilient. Reading this book is only the beginning.

As we close this section of our journey, I offer a simple technique to continue developing your future-focused leadership capabilities. This method comes from the professionals in my circle who have taught me the value of journaling. The practice I was introduced to is called "nature journaling," but I've adapted it to "natural reflections." Let's begin.

Natural Reflections

While conducting this reflective exercise in nature is ideal, any environment will work just as well. Here are the basic steps to get started.

Step One

Begin by identifying something small to observe. It could be a twig, a leaf, a pebble, or even a houseplant. Focus your full attention on this object. For each of the following prompts, it's most beneficial to say everything aloud—even if it initially feels awkward.

Prompts

- **I notice...**

  Without filters, simply state everything you observe— what you can see, feel, touch, or taste. Turn the object over and examine it from different angles. Keep repeating the phrase, "I notice..." and try to go deeper when you think you've reached the end.

- **I wonder...**

  After a period of observation, shift your attention to your curiosity. Don't worry about making perfect sense; simply state the questions or thoughts in your mind. Let your imagination and wonder guide you.

- **It reminds me of...**

  Finally, reflect out loud on what the object reminds you of. It could be memories, feelings, or connections that arise. Again, there's no need to filter yourself—let your mind wander freely.

Variations

- You can easily adapt this exercise to your journaling practice by writing down your thoughts as you speak them aloud.
- Use a photograph or image as your object of observation.
- Adapt the exercise to your existing meditation practice.
- Try drawing the object instead of describing it if you're artistically inclined.

This exercise can take as little as a few minutes. What do you notice in your immediate environment? What does it make you wonder about? What does it remind you of? This simple practice is a powerful way to strengthen your awareness, curiosity, and innovative thinking. I encourage you to create your own variation of this exercise, practice regularly, and reflect on how it influences your leadership.

Let the wisdom of the natural world guide you as you lead your teams and organizations through the complexities of today's world. Remember, leadership isn't about being untouchable or unshakeable—it's about being adaptable, open, and deeply grounded in something greater than yourself. It's about leading with intuition, resilience, and the strength that comes from understanding your place in the broader tapestry of life.

The wild is always speaking to us. Are you ready to listen?

AUTHOR BIO

John W. Sigmon is a highly regarded executive coach, speaker, and expert in organizational transformation, with a wealth of experience across various sectors of the economy. With an impressive career as a people leader and a two-time C-suite executive (CFO and CHRO), he offers unparalleled insights to help individuals and organizations create meaningful change through coaching, transformation, and tailored consulting. John uses a blend of inquiry, awareness, reflection, and action to guide his clients toward their goals.

Certified as a Master Certified Coach by the International Coach Federation (ICF) and a Master Corporate Executive Coach, John received his coach training from the prestigious Coaches Training Institute. He is also a Certified Professional Co-Active Coach and a Marshall Goldsmith Stakeholder-Centered Coach.

John works with leaders who aim to move beyond traditional leadership paradigms. He helps them embrace fearlessness, express their authentic selves, cultivate loyal followings, and engage wholeheartedly in every aspect of their lives.

www.ingramcontent.com/pod-product-compliance
Lightning Source LLC
Chambersburg PA
CBHW030849090426
42737CB00009B/1155